D1708258

MINDFUL MENTALITY

EMPATHY

BY AMBER BULLIS, MLIS

BLUE OWL
BOOKS

TIPS FOR CAREGIVERS

Social and emotional learning (SEL) helps children connect with their emotions and gain a better understanding of themselves. Mindfulness can support this learning and help them develop a kind and inclusive mentality. By incorporating mindfulness and SEL into early learning, students can establish this mentality early and be better equipped to build strong connections and communities.

BEFORE READING

Talk to the student about considering the feelings of others.

Discuss: Do you ever imagine how other people are feeling? Does it ever make you want to help them or ask them questions about why they are feeling a certain way?

AFTER READING

Talk to the student about practicing empathy.

Discuss: What does it mean to be empathetic? How will practicing empathy make you a better friend?

SEL GOAL

One way to help students become more empathetic is to help them learn to notice and listen. Try giving students a topic to discuss with each other in small groups. Those with colored popsicle sticks are the "listeners," while those with plain sticks are "sharers." Ask the listeners to repeat what they heard from the sharers. Allow each child the opportunity to practice sharing his or her opinion and listening to his or her peers.

TABLE OF CONTENTS

CHAPTER 1

WHAT IS EMPATHY?

A classmate makes fun of Tia for wearing a hijab. This hurts Tia's feelings. Her hijab is important to her. How would you feel if you were Tia?

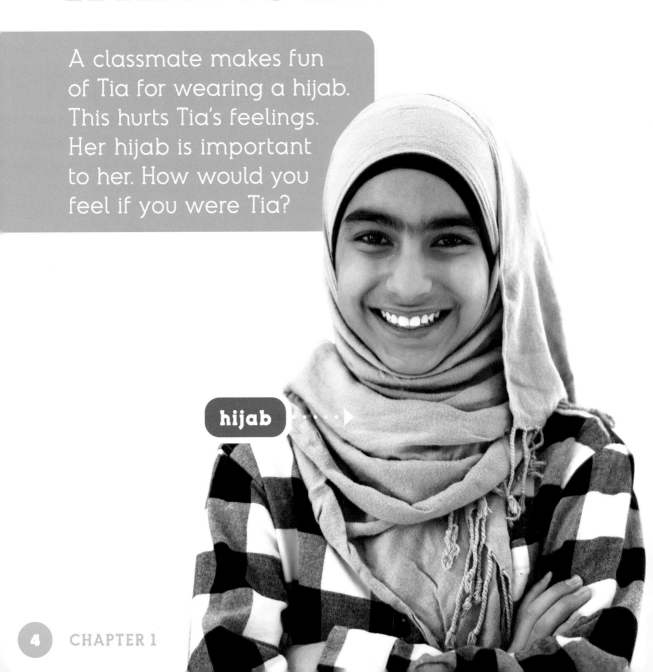

hijab ·····▶

Mel watches. She wants to make Tia feel better. She listens to Tia's feelings. This is **empathy**. Having empathy is noticing others' feelings and trying to understand them.

Empathy shows you care. There are many ways to show it! Sam helps his neighbor carry groceries.

Empathy helps us build healthy **relationships**. It also helps us be part of our **communities**. When everyone in a community feels understood, we are happier and healthier.

THE GOLDEN RULE

A good rule is to treat others the way you want to be treated. Many people call this the Golden Rule. It helps us practice empathy!

CHAPTER 2

SHOWING EMPATHY

It can be hard to show empathy when you're upset. Jake accidentally popped the soccer ball. At first, Dom gets mad. Then he pauses to take some deep breaths. He thinks about how Jake feels. He realizes it was an accident and forgives him.

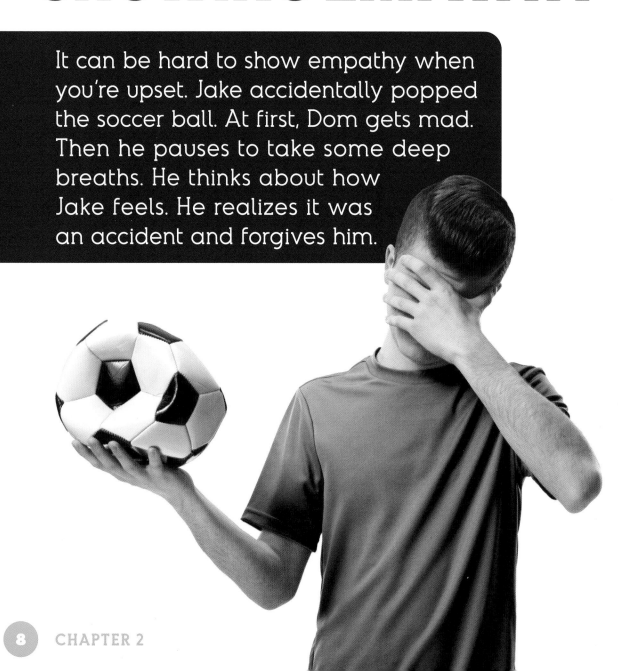

Demi got a new dog! She is smiling and laughing. Tasha smiles with her. She feels happy because her friend is happy. This is empathy, too!

Mack is sick. His family wants him to feel better, so they show empathy. How? His mom brings him more tissues. His dad makes him soup. His sister turns on his favorite movie. The next time one of his family members is sick, Mack understands. He shows them empathy, too.

Mike notices Bo sitting out. Bo has never played basketball before. Mike thinks about it from Bo's **perspective**. Maybe Bo is nervous to try. Mike understands how that feels. He **encourages** Bo to join in by helping him learn to dribble.

Kim is reading out loud in class. She reads slowly. Ellie starts to feel **impatient**. But then she remembers when she needed help with math. Kim needs extra time, just like Ellie did. Ellie decides to be respectful. After class, she tells Kim she did a good job.

USING MINDFULNESS

Mindfulness can help when you feel impatient. It can help you practice empathy, too. How? Pause. Take some deep breaths. Connect with your **emotions**.

Amelia celebrates Christmas. Her favorite tradition is decorating a tree. Tony celebrates Las Posadas. Amelia has never heard of it, so she asks Tony. She learns that it is a Mexican Christmas festival. Tony's family celebrates by breaking open a piñata. It sounds fun! Learning about it helps Amelia **appreciate** Tony's **culture**.

CELEBRATE DIFFERENCES

Everyone deserves empathy and respect. When you don't understand someone or something, ask a thoughtful question. Try to learn. It will help you empathize and understand.

?

piñata

CHAPTER 3

SHARING EMPATHY

People around you might not always show empathy. Your friend does not like the new student in your class. But he doesn't even know him. You empathize with the new student. You get to know him.

You ask him to sit with you at lunch. By doing this, you are a **role model**. You show others how to be empathetic, and you make a new friend!

Maybe you tried and still don't understand someone. Stay curious! Listen to your friends and family. Talk with them about your thoughts.

Understanding and sharing feelings can help us learn about each other and ourselves. Our communities are healthier when we understand each other.

GOALS AND TOOLS

GROW WITH GOALS

There are many ways we can learn to be more empathetic. Try these goals to practice!

Goal: Read a story about someone who is different than you. Your librarian can help you find a book you'll like.

Goal: Ask someone how they are feeling today. Listen closely to his or her words. Ask him or her questions about their feelings.

Goal: When you have a feeling, write it down. Then make a list of other words that describe that feeling.

MINDFULNESS EXERCISE

We all have similarities and differences. Identifying them and being mindful of them can help us be more empathetic.

1. On a piece of paper, make two circles that overlap in the middle. Write your name above one of them. Then write a friend's name above the other.

2. In the space where the circles overlap, write ways in which you and your friend are similar.

3. Write things that are unique to you in your circle. Then write things that are unique to your friend in the other.

4. Reflect on your similarities and differences. How can you be mindful of these? How can you be empathetic to your friend?

GLOSSARY

appreciate
To enjoy or value somebody
or something.

communities
Groups of people who all
have something in common.

culture
The ideas, customs, traditions, and
way of life of a group of people.

emotions
Feelings, such as happiness,
sadness, or anger.

empathy
The ability to understand and be
sensitive to the thoughts and feelings
of others.

encourages
Gives someone confidence, usually
by using praise and support.

impatient
Unable to put up with problems
or delays without getting angry
or upset.

mindfulness
A mentality achieved by focusing
on the present moment and calmly
recognizing and accepting your
feelings, thoughts, and sensations.

perspective
A particular attitude toward or
way of looking at something.

relationships
The ways in which people feel about
and behave toward one another, or
the ways in which two or more people
are connected.

role model
Someone whose behavior in a
certain area is imitated by others.

TO LEARN MORE

FACT SURFER

Finding more information is as easy as 1, 2, 3.

1. Go to www.factsurfer.com

2. Enter "**empathy**" into the search box.

3. Choose your cover to see a list of websites.

INDEX

Blue Owl Books are published by Jump!, 5357 Penn Avenue South, Minneapolis, MN 55419, www.jumplibrary.com

Library of Congress Cataloging-in-Publication Data is available at www.loc.gov or upon request from the publisher.

Names: Bullis, Amber, author.
Title: Empathy / Amber Bullis.
Description: Minneapolis: Jump!, Inc., 2021. | Series: Mindful mentality
Includes index. | Audience: Ages 7–10 | Audience: Grades 2–3
Identifiers: LCCN 2020013528 (print)
LCCN 2020013529 (ebook)
ISBN 9781645273776 (hardcover)
ISBN 9781645273783 (paperback)
ISBN 9781645273790 (ebook)
Subjects: LCSH: Empathy–Juvenile literature. | Mindfulness (Psychology)–Juvenile literature.
Classification: LCC BF575.E55 B85 2021 (print)
LCC BF575.E55 (ebook) | DDC 155.4/1241–dc23
LC record available at https://lccn.loc.gov/2020013528
LC ebook record available at https://lccn.loc.gov/2020013529

Editor: Jenna Gleisner
Designer: Molly Ballanger

Photo Credits: Prostock-studio/Shutterstock, cover; LightField Studios/Shutterstock, 1, 3; FatCamera/iStock, 4, 5, 14–15; eclipse_images/iStock, 6–7; Ljupco Smokovski/ Shutterstock, 8; Vesnaandjic/iStock, 9; Prostock-studio/iStock, 10–11; cyano66/iStock, 12–13; aldomurillo/iStock, 16–17; Pixel-Shot/Shutterstock, 18, 19; Don Mason/Getty, 20–21.

Printed in the United States of America at Corporate Graphics in North Mankato, Minnesota.